?
what's your excuse
for not
getting your dream job

what's your excuse ...

FOR NOT GETTING YOUR DREAM JOB?

Overcome your excuses and make
your move to a happier working life

rosemary lemon

"Optimistic, realistic and written with clarity, this book is filled to the brim with bite-sized, practical suggestions on how to overcome fears and worries to make your dream job become a reality. Readers should feel their confidence grow as they move toward a happier, more fulfilled working life"

John Raftery, vice chancellor, London Metropolitan University

"An easy to read book that strikes a good balance between providing helpful hints and tips and prompting the reader to consider exactly what is preventing them from getting their dream job"

Stuart Hannan, Inspired Decisions Ltd

"In this timely and topical publication, Rosemary offers valuable and practical insights from her many years of experience in the changing world of work. Finding a new job can be a daunting experience but with thought, preparation and persistence it can be made easier. Rosemary examines each key stage of the job search process in a clear and succinct style"

Doug Evans, group legal counsel, Hays plc

"Almost half of the workforce now want to work for an organisation that has a positive impact on the world alongside a good work-life balance. Rosemary Lemon provides a simple, practical and thoughtful

guide for anyone driven to make that a reality. Dare to live the life you have dreamed for yourself"

Daniel Shakhani, founder, SalaryFinance

"Nowadays more and more people want a job that lets them be themselves, empowers them to grow and is challenging and fun. This book is full of useful advice. Rosemary Lemon provides practical guidance based on her vast experience in recruitment and encourages readers to do some self-analysis and to stop living a life of 'if onlys'. This book is so easy to read that it is like having a conversation with a mentor or a very good friend who will help you to look at where you are in your career, identify your dream job and work out the actions you need to take to get it"

Laura Vanessa Munoz, founder, Empowering Futures

"If you are in any way unhappy with your job or career choice this book gives you a simple, straightforward but comprehensive methodology to help you determine what is the right job for you by helping you to better understand what makes you happy, and it then provides a series of practical steps to the perfect job. With the maxim that if you are going to spend forty years at work, you should make sure they are enjoyable ones!"

Paul Venables, CFO, Hays Plc

Also in this series

Clearing Your Clutter
Being More Productive
Living a Life You Love
Being Successful as an Artist
Getting Fit
Overcoming Stress
Being Better With Money
Loving Your Job
Eating Healthily
Being More Confident

What's Your Excuse for not Getting Your Dream Job?

This first edition published in 2018 by WYE Publishing
9 Evelyn Gardens, Richmond TW9 2PL
www.wyepublishing.com

Copyright © Rosemary Lemon 2018

Rosemary Lemon asserts her moral right to be identified as the author of this book

ISBN 978-0-9956052-8-2

Cover and text design by Annette Peppis & Associates

Printed and bound in Great Britain by
Marston Book Services Ltd, Oxfordshire

All rights reserved. No part of this publication may be reproduced, stored in a retrieval system or transmitted in any form or by any means, electronic, mechanical, photocopying, recording or otherwise, without the prior permission of the publishers

'What's Your Excuse…?' is a UK Registered Trade Mark
(Registration No: 3018995)

www.whatsyourexcuse.co.uk
Follow What's Your Excuse…? on Twitter – @whats_yr_excuse
www.facebook.com/whatsyourexcusebooks

Contents

Introduction — 13
How this book will help you — 13
Why follow your dream? — 16
What can happen if you don't follow your dream? — 18
How to use this book — 19

The Excuses — 21
Getting Started — 23
I'm too busy with my current job to look for a new one — 23
I don't know what my dream job would be — 23
If my current job could be improved it would be my dream role — 27
I don't know where to look for vacancies — 30

Fears — 35
I'm frightened of failure — 35
I'm too old — 36
I'm too young — 41
It's too risky — 43
I tried it before and didn't succeed — 45

Skills and Qualifications	**51**
I don't have the right experience	51
I don't have the right skills	54
I don't have the right qualifications	56
I don't know the right people	59
What I currently do has no relevance	63
I have been out of the workplace for too long	66
The Application	**69**
I don't have any time to complete the application	69
Applying for jobs is tedious	70
I don't know how to write a CV	71
I don't know how to write a covering letter	76
I'll do it tomorrow	79
The Interview	**81**
I don't know what to wear	81
I get tongue-tied and don't know what to say	82
I get so nervous	85
I don't know how to reply when they ask if I have anything else to add	88
I don't know what to say when they ask if I have any questions	89
I find it hard to sell myself	91

Finances	**93**
I can't afford to retrain	93
My dream job won't pay enough	94
Getting the Job	**99**
I'm worried about what other people might think of me	99
Is it OK to compromise?	100

Some Final Thoughts 103

Acknowledgements 109

About the Author 111

Index 113

Introduction

How this book will help you

Are you stuck in a job you don't enjoy? Are you looking for a career change but you're not sure if it's possible? Are you at the start of your career but don't feel confident that the job you really want is actually achievable?

I've written this book to help you explore and plan a route to your perfect role, and to explain how even a major career change can be possible with the right approach and persistence.

There will be obstacles to overcome, and these can often be of our own making in the form of excuses, but this book addresses all of the most common excuses I've heard during my time working in human resources and gives you advice and guidance on how to overcome them.

The fact is you *can* overcome your own excuses and take action. The aim of this book is to give you a better understanding of how to do that, so that you don't spend your life doing work you don't enjoy.

Why follow your dream?

I strongly believe in following your dreams. If there is something you really and truly want to do, it is important to try to achieve it. You only have one life and it is important to spend that life being happy, pursuing the things you love and having no regrets.

If your dream is a particular job, then I believe you should pursue that dream. It may take some time and you may have to overcome some obstacles but you've probably heard the saying, 'Choose a job you love and you will never have to work a day in your life'.

The fact is that most of us will have to work for at least forty years, if not more. That is half a lifetime! If we are going to spend fifty percent our lives at work it makes sense to spend it in a job we enjoy.

Here are some of the benefits of being happy in your work:

- You'll look forward to your work and feel positive about starting your day
- You won't spend the day clock-watching or feeling bored

- You will have a sense of satisfaction and have pride in your achievements
- You'll have fewer regrets when you reflect back in later life
- You'll be productive and achieve more, which means you will be more successful

When you're happy and enthusiastic about your work you will find that your general energy levels will increase and you will feel better about yourself. When you have positive feelings in one area of your life they spill out and improve other areas: health, family, relationships, everything. Enjoying your job is an important element of your overall wellbeing.

What can happen if you don't follow your dream?

Years spent in work you don't enjoy will take their toll:

- You'll dread Mondays
- You'll feel unfulfilled
- You'll be bored
- You won't produce your best work and won't reach your potential
- If you're not producing your best work you won't stand out and might miss out on opportunities for advancement and recognition

Spending your time in work you don't enjoy will have a negative impact on how you feel generally and your levels of energy and enthusiasm outside of work may suffer. This may impact your health and relationships, but most of all you may one day regret spending so much time in a job you didn't enjoy.

How to use this book

You can read this book cover to cover or you can dip into it and read the chapters which are most relevant to you.

The book is structured around some key themes and the concerns you might have about pursuing your dream job. Many of our fears and worries show up as excuses and for each excuse I give some useful information and suggestions on how to overcome it.

Everyone has different reasons or excuses for not doing things so don't feel bad or guilty about your own – you are not alone! This book will give you manageable and practical advice on overcoming the things which may be holding you back from a happier working life. Tackle them one at a time, feel your confidence grow and enjoy moving closer to your dream role.

The Excuses

Getting Started

I'm too busy with my current job to look for a new one

When you are at work it is very easy to feel overloaded; it is often hard to say no to colleagues or managers particularly when they all believe their piece of work is the most urgent! In this situation the key to finding time for your own job search is to know how to prioritise.

If you are able to prioritise well, then you will be able to ascertain whether something really needs doing straight away, later or indeed whether it really needs doing at all. Sometimes we can find ourselves feeling so busy that we forget to question why something is needed or to think of a new and more efficient way of doing it. If you are organised enough to know exactly what you have on your to-do list and you can prioritise then you will be able to juggle your tasks more effectively and create time to focus on other things. Organised people tend to be more productive. This applies not only to people at work but to those who juggle family commitments, have lots of hobbies and interests, sit on committees, volunteer to do charity work or pursue other activities outside of work.

One way of organising and setting priorities is to group everything you have to do into these categories:

- Important and urgent – do these first
- Important but not urgent – you may be able to postpone these to a time when you are less busy, or delegate them
- Not important and not urgent – ask yourself if these really need doing at all! Sometimes we can end up doing something just because it has always been done when actually it has become unnecessary. Even if these type of tasks do need doing they can be last on your list and possibly postponed indefinitely

Organising your tasks like this will help you to see where you might be able to find some time. Remember, in work and life generally, priorities change all the time so you need to review your list regularly.

Finally think about the category into which your job search falls – if it is in the first one you should be prioritising it accordingly!

You might also want to take a look at Juliet Landau-Pope's book "What's Your Excuse for not being More Productive?" for more on time management.[1]

---

[1] Juliet Landau-Pope, What's Your Excuse for not Being More Productive? WYE Publishing, 2017

I don't know what my dream job would be

A recruitment consultant once approached an employee and told him that he could help him to take his next step in getting to the top of his career. The employee answered that he didn't need any help as he was already where he wanted to be. The recruitment consultant was confused – the employee wasn't anywhere near the top of the management chain and there was plenty of opportunity for further progression. However the employee replied, 'I enjoy meeting and selling to my customers, I am paid enough that I don't need to worry about my rent and I can afford to go on holiday. I finish work at five o'clock every day and get back in time to see my children. I am not stressed about my job in the evening, I like my work colleagues, I am in a great office with a convenient journey home. I am just where I want to be; I have my dream job'.

> Dream jobs may not always have a specific job title

I love this story. It shows that dream jobs may not always have a specific job title or necessarily be high status but may comprise a number of elements, benefits or attributes – your colleagues, your commute, your working environment – which give you the lifestyle and enjoyment you want.

So don't worry if you don't have a title for your dream job. What's more important is that you find a role which ticks all of your boxes in terms of job satisfaction, level of responsibility, remuneration and environment.

It is therefore worth making a list of what you are really looking for when you think of your dream role – is it a different kind of work, a different kind of lifestyle or a combination? This is a bit like describing the house you're looking for to an estate agent: number of bedrooms, size of garden, type of neighbourhood, etc. If your dream job doesn't have a specific job title, then list all of the attributes you are looking for and this will give you a better idea of next steps – it could be you can look at enhancing your own job (see the next chapter for more on this) or perhaps consider working more flexibly to change your lifestyle. Alternatively, if you need to look for a brand new role, then you will have a very good idea of the key attributes you are looking for when searching for vacancies or speaking to recruitment agencies.

If my current job could be improved it would be my dream role

If there are elements of your job which you like and which you'd like to do more of or if you think your job would be improved if you could get involved in other activities, it's worth exploring this.

Talk to your manager – you don't need to wait until a formal appraisal or career development meeting. Ask for a chat, explain what you love doing and ask how you could develop into a role where you do more of it. Managers love enthusiasm and they love employees who want to take on more responsibility. A good manager will help you to develop.

> The more you demonstrate how good you are, the more your reputation will grow

Make it known throughout your company what you enjoy doing. When you've enjoyed working on a particular piece of work, tell colleagues. If you've done it well then the next time a similar piece of work comes up they will think of you. The more you demonstrate how good you are, the more your reputation will grow.

Seek out projects which will allow you the scope to do the things you enjoy. For example, if you love presenting to people, go and talk to the people responsible for training or sales. You might get the chance to help with training, to shadow someone during a sales event or to promote the company at a conference. The more you tell people about what you like doing, the more they will think of you when opportunities arise.

This is what is often referred to as building a personal brand. The reason that there is a difference in cost between a plain white tee shirt and one with a big brand logo is to do with what is associated with that brand: quality, customer service, innovation, etc. Big, respected brands are in demand and attract higher prices and that is what you should be aiming at for yourself – getting noticed for all the right reasons and increasing your saleability and the demand for what you offer.

In my past I built up a reputation for being reliable and well-organised – it was part of my personal brand. This paid off when the CEO of one of the companies I worked for announced that he wanted to set up a project to raise money for charities supporting children with HIV/AIDS in South Africa. Because he was aware of my work in other areas and he knew that I had always wanted to get involved in projects which would make a difference, when I asked if I could help he invited me to run the project. It was a fabulous experience and one of the most special things I have done, all thanks to my reputation and personal brand.

One word of warning on your current job though: even if it has some great elements you are still likely to have to do tasks you don't like. All jobs have some boring bits and if you don't get the basic parts of your job done well, no one is going to help you to do more of the parts you love. Therefore show how efficient you are by getting those less interesting bits of the job done and out of the way so that you have the time to devote to what you really want to do. For example, set aside an hour each morning to process invoices or stock-take or clean (or whatever it is that you find tedious). You are fresher in the morning and it will take less time to get through these routine tasks. Get them out of the way and then the rest of the day is yours to concentrate on the most fun parts of your job.

If you do want to stay put you might also want to take a look at Amanda Cullen's book "What's Your Excuse for not Loving Your Job?" for more advice.[2]

---

2 Amanda Cullen, *What's Your Excuse for not Loving Your Job?* WYE Publishing, 2016

I don't know where to look for vacancies

There are a number of traditional places you can look for vacancies:

Specialist recruitment agencies
Many companies ask recruitment agents to handle their recruitment. Once you make contact it's important to keep in touch with them and build relationships with them. If you are there in the forefront of their mind, they will think of you when that dream position comes along.

Recruitment agencies use LinkedIn so make sure you have a LinkedIn profile and keep it up to date – see more on LinkedIn in "I don't know the right people".

To find relevant agencies, use an online directory such as CV Library.[3]

Specialist publications
There are publications, magazines and websites for just about every industry and very often specialist roles will be advertised in them. You may be able to find them by searching the web. Sometimes companies will display magazines which relate to their industry in their foyers or shops – you may find a publication

---

3   https://www.cv-library.co.uk/companies/agencies

you'd like to subscribe to or a free company brochure to take away. Even if there are no jobs advertised in these publications you can read more about the company and gain valuable knowledge about the industry. For some larger companies you may find you have to get past general security but if you say you are looking for some company literature and are not progressing past the general reception area, you will usually be successful; you are only asking for a brochure and companies love to give out literature!

Company websites

Some companies advertise roles on their website. If there is a company you'd particularly like to work for keep an eye on their website. Sign up to automatic email alerts if you can and sign up to their newsletter. That way you'll be aware of any relevant news about the company. For example, if a company is relocating not all of their employees may relocate with them which may result in them having some vacancies. If you get advance notice of the relocation, you will be able to contact them about possible opportunities before the jobs are even advertised.

There are also some less traditional ways of finding out about vacancies which can be very effective:

Word of mouth

If you build up a network of contacts you may hear about possible vacancies from them. If people with whom you have built up positive relationships know you are interested in a certain type of position they will keep an eye open for you and let you know if they hear of something. Often in large companies jobs are advertised internally and so any contacts you have in the industry in which you want to work may hear about them first and let you know about vacancies before they are advertised externally. Remember also that friends and colleagues may also have their own networks and if you let them know what your ambitions are they can spread the word further to an even wider network. I can't emphasise enough the importance of building good, strong, positive relationships with as many people as possible – see more about this in "I don't know the right people".

Proactive contact

There is no harm in actually just contacting a company, explaining the type of role you are looking for and asking if they have any opportunities. You never know what may happen. They may be thinking of hiring but just haven't yet advertised; they may love your CV, think you are exactly the kind of person they want to employ and so create a role; or they may hold your CV on file and contact you if an opportunity arises in the future. If they don't have anything suitable and are not hiring you are no worse off than before – you'll not have lost anything and on the positive side you'll have raised your profile and had practice at selling yourself.

Headhunters

If you're hoping to be headhunted, be realistic. In order for this to happen you need to be well-known in the marketplace, you need to have built a reputation for being good at what you want to do and have proven skills. As I have already said building a good network is important so see "I don't know the right people" for advice on creating an effective network of contacts who can spread the word of your reputation.

Finally, you don't have to try these options one at a time – use as many as possible to give yourself the greatest chance of finding your dream job.

Fears

I'm frightened of failure

Many people have a fear of the unknown. It is easy to think of all the things which might go wrong and to feel so panicked by them that you don't dare to do anything.

What is the worst thing that could happen? You may not get the first job you apply for but you'd be no worse off than you are now. You won't have lost the job you have. What's more, you can become wiser by learning from your experiences. In human resources we are fond of saying that when things go wrong they are not failures but learning opportunities. If you learn from your mistakes, it will make you better prepared for next time.

I used to worry about everything when I was younger. My mum used to say, 'Today is the tomorrow you worried about yesterday and all is well'. Most things you fret about won't happen, and even if they do they are often not nearly so bad as you'd imagined.

Identify what is scaring you and then work out what you can do to mitigate it. Good planning will help you to identify what might go wrong and to do something to prevent it.

List your worries and then categorise them into those you can influence and those you can't. Let go of the things about which you can do nothing and concentrate on those things you *can* influence. Worrying about things over which you have no control is a waste of energy. For instance, there is no point in getting anxious about how qualified other candidates may be; it is better to focus on how best to sell the qualifications and skills you have.

> Concentrate on those things you can influence

You will find that once you've addressed the things you can influence, other worries will diminish or disappear; you will have grown in confidence by tackling the things over which you have control and this will help you to put other worries in perspective.

I'm too old

You are never too old! And there are a number of very positive aspects to being older:

You have lots of experience
You will have gained common sense and a lot of life

and work experience over the years, even if not yet in the area you are hoping to work in. All jobs call for some transferrable skills: abilities which can apply to many roles (see "What I currently do has no relevance" for more on these). Examples of transferrable skills are good organisation, the ability to explain things clearly, a good telephone manner, being able to write a report, to deal calmly when customers are upset or to keep calm in a crisis. Your transferrable skills are likely to be better than the skills of people just starting out on their career because you have had more time to hone them.

You have grativas

There is also something about having a bit of grey hair to add gravitas to what you say and do. Maturity adds weight to what you have to say. This means that even if your dream job is utterly different to what you have done before the fact that you are older shows that you are more likely to have thought it through and that you will understand what you are taking on.

> Maturity adds weight to what you have to say

A recruitment manager for a large global company was looking for someone to lead their graduate recruitment programme. Initially she thought that someone with a couple of years' work experience following graduation might be suitable as they could relate to the student intake. One of the applicants however was much more mature. This candidate was full of enthusiasm; her own children were grown up and she had watched them take on graduate positions and understood what the positions involved. She admitted that she would have to learn some new skills but was really interested in the role. She was offered the job and she turned out to be superb at it.

In addition the decision makers in an organisation – those people who you'll be aiming to impress at interview – are also likely to be older. It can help a lot with your confidence when you are talking to or being interviewed by someone who is your peer in terms of age or life experience.

I can write about this from a personal perspective. I work with directors on often sensitive people issues and when I started out in my twenties I was speaking to people who were in their fifties. This can make a real difference when trying to relate to someone on a life experience basis, especially when dealing with personal issues. In my job now, I am the same age as the people who sit on our board and it makes for a subtly different dynamic. While they are in a more senior position, we are at ease with each other as we have been through the same learning curves and experiences.

Age is only skin deep

Remember the saying 'You are only as old as you feel'. This is important – if you feel young and vibrant inside, it will show on the outside. If you have enthusiasm it will shine through. When I am recruiting people, I know that having someone who really wants to do well, is willing to learn, is really interested in what they want to do and is enthusiastic counts for a lot. I would rather employ someone who has the right attitude but who needs some training than a person with all the right skills but no enthusiasm.

You're not the first

Academics have researched the success rates of people switching careers in later life. A study on new careers for older workers carried out by the American Institute for Economic Research found that out of the older adults who attempted to change career, most were successful:

> 'AIER found that late-in-life career changes affect millions of people. In fact, our survey, given sampling error, found that anywhere from 16 million to 29 million people attempted a career change after age 45. Moreover, 82 percent of late-in-career changers were successful'[4]

---

4   https://www.aier.org/sites/default/files/Files/WYSIWYG/page/4837/newcareersolderworkers-aier.pdf

This is encouraging!

And there are some famous examples of people who changed direction in later life:

- Vera Wang was a figure skater and journalist and didn't start her fashion career until she was forty. Today she is one of the world's top designers

- Harland Sanders had a restaurant and motel in Kentucky but when a new interstate opened seven miles from his restaurant in 1952 his business began to flag. Rather than give up he went to work on developing a spice and quick cooking technique for fried chicken. He then toured the country selling Kentucky Fried Chicken franchises and in 1964, when he had over nine hundred franchises, he sold his business for two million dollars. He was sixty-five

- Actor Ricky Tomlinson worked as a plasterer and spent years as a political activist before getting his first acting role in Boys from the Blackstuff at the age of forty-two

- At the age of fifty-five after a career in acting Ronald Reagan was elected as Governor of California, which led to him becoming President of the United States at the age of almost seventy

Finally, remember that you don't have to put your age on your CV. It is illegal to discriminate on age and your date of birth is irrelevant when applying for a job. Your future employer is obliged to judge you on your abilities, not your age. Once you are actually in front of a prospective employer, you have the ability to shine and make your case as to why they should employ you. Age does not come into it.

Age is no longer a barrier. People are living longer and staying healthier. We go through many stages in our lives and we develop and grow all the time. There is absolutely no reason at all why you shouldn't decide to have a go at something else later in life.

I'm too young

We all have to start somewhere and anyone who now has a job had to get on the first rung of the career ladder. This includes people who are recruiting so they will understand if you may have limited experience.

However, there are steps you can take to help yourself:

- Use your free time to get some work experience. While it would be great if you were able to get an internship this may not be possible, but try voluntary work or ask to work for free in a local company for a few days. The most important thing is to demonstrate that you have used your time wisely to gain whatever experience you can. It will show that you understand the basics of working life: reliability, organisation, working in a team, punctuality and dressing appropriately. It will also show that you want to learn. Faced with two similar candidates, one who has spent the summer holidays working and one who has done nothing but watch TV, I know which one I am more interested in

- Identify your transferrable skills (see "What I currently do is of no relevance"). You may have gained these through hobbies or school or university activities. Work out how you can relate them to the job for which you are applying

- Research any company you are hoping to work for and its strategy so that you can demonstrate knowledge and understanding of some of the issues within the industry even if you haven't got direct experience. A company's annual report is a great place to start – it should be written in everyday language and have specific sections on its business focus. You will find this on their website, usually in the investor section

- Be sensible about the jobs you apply for. For instance, you are unlikely to get a job as a manager if you have never worked before or have had little or no experience – be humble and realistic and start in a role from where you can learn and grow

Applying for a job is about selling yourself to an employer. By identifying your transferrable skills and how these can relate to your dream job and by showing you have carefully researched the industry and know something about the company you will demonstrate to your prospective employer that you are motivated, interested in learning more and have the potential to do the job. The fact that you have thought it through carefully in this way may give you the edge on other candidates applying for the role. Take a look at "The Application" section for more advice on this.

It's worth remembering too that if you are bold and imaginative you could simply create your own dream role:

- Zoe 'Zoella' Sugg was a trainee in an interior design company when she decided to start a lifestyle blog in 2009, at the age of nineteen. It developed into a YouTube channel and she now has an enormous global following on social media and a book deal. In 2013 at the age of twenty-three she was named as one of Britain's most influential tweeters by The Telegraph[5]

- At the age of ten Henry Patterson wrote a children's book which, when it was published in 2014 sold thousands of copies. The Not Before Tea website followed, selling gifts based on characters from his book[6]

- At twenty-five James Gupta is already setting up a second business after developing a taxi sharing app while at university and selling it to Addison Lee[7]

What these young people all have in common is harnessing technology to reach a huge audience without too much investment. You might want to consider how new online tools could help you develop your own dream role.

---

5 https://www.zoella.co.uk
6 http://www.notbeforetea.co.uk
7 https://startups.co.uk/young-entrepreneurs-james-gupta-synap

It's too risky

If you are a naturally cautious person you may imagine all sorts of risks. We can also get very set in our ways so if you have worked in your current job for a long time the idea of leaving everything you are familiar with to step into something you may never have done before may well feel scary. But if you're too cautious you run the risk of doing nothing!

There are really two types of job move: one within the same industry which involves the skills you already have and the things you currently enjoy doing, and one which involves a change of direction and a brand new set of skills. The first type is less risky as you are already part of the way there; you are already doing many of the things you enjoy and you already know the industry so you have less to learn and there is less risk. The second type is the one which will feel scarier.

> If you're too cautious you run the risk of doing nothing

You can plan for and mitigate risk. Start by doing a risk assessment. Make a list of what you consider to be the risks in your planned career change and categorise them as follows:

- High impact and likely to happen – these are the risks you need to manage most carefully
- Low impact and likely to happen – consider what you can do to mitigate these but if they do happen and they are not going to have a serious impact then how much do you need to worry?
- High impact but unlikely to happen – your imagination may be doing overtime! Look at these only if you can truly say your concerns are realistic
- Low impact and unlikely to happen – put these to one side and stop worrying!

The risks in the first and second categories are the ones you should tackle and plan for. Hopefully you can relax a little about the ones in the third and fourth categories – even if the risks in the fourth category did happen the impact wouldn't be great.

As an example of how to plan for a risk, let's say you consider it a great risk that you won't perform well in the job you're applying for. What can you do to mitigate this? You could ensure that you fully understand the role and

> If you don't try, you may always regret it

what it entails before you apply so that there will be no surprises if you do get chosen, you can ensure that you ask the right questions at interview to get a clear understanding of the company's expectations and you could brush up on particular skills where you think you might be rusty.

By assessing and addressing risks in this way they should feel less overwhelming and you can focus your efforts in the right place.

Of course there is one other risk you should consider – the risk that if you don't try, you may always regret it. Wouldn't it be better to say that you gave it your best shot? You don't want to look back and think 'if only…'

I tried it before and didn't succeed

That was then and this is now. Just because you didn't succeed last time doesn't mean you won't ever. Rather than feeling despondent about past experiences, reframe them as learning opportunities and as part of a journey. If you understand what happened in the past then you can do something differently this time around. Ask yourself:

- Were you daunted by the qualifications needed and therefore didn't give it your best shot?
- Were you unprepared for the interview?
- Did you not have enough experience at the time?

- Did you let other people discourage you?
- Did you not have enough time to properly research the company?
- What other set-backs did you encounter?

Once you've analysed what went wrong last time you can put together a plan of action: what you need to do to avoid the same things happening again, how you are going to do it and who can help you.

For example:

I had to demonstrate how I would sell a product to a client – I stumbled through my words as I wasn't sure how to structure my sales pitch and I didn't know how to prepare a professional presentation.

What you need to do: *I need to learn presentation skills as my dream job will require me to sell a product. I need to learn Powerpoint and learn how to structure what I am going to say.*

How will you do it: *I will book myself some Powerpoint training. I will ask if I can attend a sales presentation and I will ask if I can practise by presenting to colleagues.*

Who might help me? *The sales team at work might*

help me and I have friends who do presentations all the time who may also be willing to give me some tips. I will look for advice online.

Remember that most things are doable but in order to do them you have also to make them manageable. Breaking things down into small chunks makes them easier to tackle and less daunting and overwhelming. Organisation is a skill in itself – employers will be impressed if you have so much enthusiasm for a role that you have methodically tried everything to achieve it.

Don't forget to celebrate your successes along the way and recognise what you have achieved. You are moving closer to that new job!

Skills and Qualifications

I don't have the right experience

This must feel like a catch twenty-two situation – how can anyone get any job if they have no experience? However at some point in our lives we all got our first job and it can happen again for you in a completely different field. Get clever and find creative ways of making it happen.

Start with speaking to your friends and colleagues - your network. When you start to talk to people about their passions and interests or previous jobs and experience you'll be amazed at how much talent and knowledge they have and how diverse their experience is. When I've chatted to colleagues previously, I concluded that we had the skills to set up a new and entirely different business. Even friends take me by surprise: a friend in the recruitment business casually let on to me recently that during her twenties she had volunteered to work in some of Australia's most notorious prisons as a warder during a period of strikes. You never know how the people you know or the people they know might be able to help you until you share your dream and ask about their experience, knowledge and contacts.

For instance, my daughter is passionate about environmental protection and wants to have a career where she can influence these issues, without having a specific job title in mind. Within my network I have been able to put her in touch with someone who heads a charity protecting the Galapagos Islands, someone who helps form environmental policy in Wales and people who work in waste management.

> Use your friends and contacts

Use your friends and contacts and tell them what you're hoping to do. Friends may know friends who know friends who work in the area you are interested in and may be able to help. Join networking groups that specialise in the area you are interested in and talk to the members about getting experience. Offer to volunteer to work for free to see what it is like and gain that valuable hands-on experience you need.

You can also create your own experience. Call into local businesses and ask if you can volunteer to help them for a day – if necessary take a day's leave from your current job to do so. You might be surprised at what you learn and your enthusiasm may lead to bigger and better things!

Consider organising your own events. If you want to break into fashion, organise your own fashion show – ask local clothes shops if they will participate and ask your friends to be models. If you make it a charity event people may be more willing to get involved. You'll gain experience of organisation, advertising, selling, dealing with the public, handling money and putting together outfits plus, if you enjoy it, you'll be able to talk about it in an engaging and enthusiastic manner in the future.

If you are in work already is there an opportunity to get involved with a project that would give you the experience you need? When you next meet with your manager talk about the areas of your personal development you would most like to work on. Most managers are delighted to hear you want to progress or develop and will be pleased to help you. If you have some positive ideas of what you could do then suggest them.

> Enthusiasm and reliability will count for a lot

Try to think outside of the box when considering how you could gain some experience of the things that you'd love to be doing as a job in the future.

Finally, employers publish a wish list of experience when they advertise jobs but you shouldn't be put off if you can't tick every box. They will often specify what is really essential to them and the rest is just 'nice to haves'. Remember you can always learn, and your enthusiasm and reliability will count for a lot!

I don't have the right skills

You can learn new skills by practising on the job or by going on a training course.

Here are some ways you can develop new skills:

In your current job:
- If your ideal job needs proficiency in, say, coding, then could what you do now be enhanced if you learned it? If so, your company may fund some training
- Many computer-based applications are intuitive and straightforward to use. Don't be afraid of having a go and trying things out in a quiet moment
- Find an expert colleague. People feel flattered when they are asked for help or when someone acknowledges them as being an expert in what they do. Most people are more than happy to assist if you pick a convenient moment

Outside of work:
- If you are looking to develop practical skills like

gardening or cake decoration, then could you volunteer for a charity or offer to help at a school event? Are any of your friends involved with organisations or associations where you could assist? This is a great way of finding opportunities to practise skills in a relatively safe environment
- Take a look at YouTube. You'll find a wide variety of tutorials and practical demonstrations to guide you in your learning

On formal training courses:
- If the skill you need is specific and won't require a long period of study, then you should be able to find a course at an adult college. You can search on line for an appropriate course.[8] For a few hours a week you can learn with people at the same level as you, learn from each other and laugh at your mistakes together. You will also form a network of contacts to call upon if you need some help in the future
- If the skill you need is more involved or needs to lead to a formal qualification it will obviously require a greater level of commitment, both in time and financially. Look up your local college online and download their prospectus. Colleges will be able to offer advice on available grants or loans, but see

---

8   Try https://www.hotcourses.com

also "I can't afford to retrain" for ideas on how to fund this type of training

If you do learn something new, put it to use straight away. Practising a new skill in a real situation helps to embed it in your mind. It will also give you real examples of how you have used your skills when applying for jobs.

I don't have the right qualifications

Some roles do require specific qualifications, for instance medicine, electrical work or law, and these can require long periods of education and study.

If committing several years to studying is not possible for you there may still be other ways of obtaining a qualification. For example, I studied French at university and after working in various sales, marketing and strategic planning roles I moved to human resources. The main recognised qualification in human resources is the CIPD and most employers look for this.[9] Rather than study full time or in the evenings over a three year period, I looked for another route and found that I could achieve this through professional assessment, which allows you

---

9 *Chartered Institute of Personnel & Development*

to be assessed on actually doing the work rather than studying the theory. You do this by providing evidence of acquired knowledge and experience via documents you have written or statements from managers or feedback from employees. This took intensive effort but I managed to do it in five and a half months.

So when it comes to qualifications, try to think outside of the box – are there ways of getting the certification you need other than the traditional full-time study route?

- If you can join a company at a junior level, will they train you while you work? Many employers, such as accountants, law firms, hairdressers and construction companies, offer on-the-job training or apprenticeships

- Think about some of the experiences you have had and check exactly what the qualification involves – you may be exempt from some modules because of your past experience, even if it is in another field

- As for obtaining specific qualifications, consider evening classes.[10] These can vary from getting certification in practical trades such as electrical work, construction or cookery to business studies

---

10 https://www.hotcourses.com

and language skills and GCSEs and A Levels. A few hours' study per week may secure you that dream role eventually if you are patient

- Consider the Open University or U3A (University of the Third Age) who both offer courses you can do in your own time[11]

You might also want to consider contacting a company or an association related to your ideal role and ask for their advice on how to get qualified. When people specialise in a certain industry they will know exactly how to go about getting the qualifications and skills you need – you may be surprised at the choices available to you.

If the role you want demands it you have no choice but to do formal training and it may need time, dedication and commitment but there is usually more than one way of achieving something and it will be worth it if it helps you to secure the role you really want.

---

11 http://www.open.ac.uk/courses, https://u3a.org.uk

I don't know the right people

There will always be someone who can help you. You just need to find them. This is where networking is so important. Networking is the art of meeting and building relationships with a wide variety of people so that you can share experiences, learn and support each other.

Here are some of the best ways to build your own network:

- **Use LinkedIn**

    Make sure you have an up to date, detailed profile on LinkedIn. It is your online CV. Recruiters will search LinkedIn when looking for candidates. Crucially, it is also the place to find like-minded people and you can invite them to connect with you. You can write them a note when you invite them to connect to explain your interest in their industry and ask if they would be willing to give you any hints or tips on what to do. Most people are flattered to be asked for their views or advice (rather than a job). If you can't find a relevant person, post a request for advice or help. You may be surprised at the response.

    Join LinkedIn groups too, and post your own articles and blogs. Your photo and everything you say will be available for other professionals to see, including those who may be useful contacts in your search for your ideal role, so be professional!

- **Attend conferences and seminars**
  Every profession or industry has a whole network of specialists and conferences and seminars are a good place to meet them. Many of these are free to attend. You can learn about the latest developments in the industry or profession but more importantly use them as an opportunity to meet people working in the sort of job you want

- **Join professional networks and associations**
  All professions and industries have their own associations. If you can't find out about these for yourself, ask someone on LinkedIn. Joining an appropriate association will give you access to a wealth of resources and contacts who may be able to help you

- **Friends of friends**
  Ask your friends and trusted colleagues if they know of anyone you can talk to. Everyone has their own network – family, friends, friends of friends, colleagues, professional contacts, suppliers, etc. Someone will know someone who may be able to

point you in the right direction or offer you guidance and help

- **Make your own contacts**
  Are there any local businesses close to you that you'd like to work for? Many small companies have their own website or feature on social media so if you don't know of one, search online. Contact them to ask if you could chat to someone and get some advice on how to get started. You could even ask if you could work for free for a day. While local, smaller businesses may be more flexible than larger companies, there is nothing to stop you doing the same with larger organisations. Remember that you are not asking for a job; you are simply building up your network of contacts. Of course if you do get the opportunity to visit them, you also have the opportunity to showcase who you are and what you can offer and should there be a vacancy in the future you never know what might happen, but at the very least, you can add the people you meet to your network

- **Get noticed on social media**
  Post articles or a blog on aspects of your dream job – this will show you know something about it! Articles on LinkedIn are especially important as

recruiters may notice you there. Make sure your articles are factual and if you state a personal view, think about what impact it will have and whether it projects the right image before you post it

- **Get a mentor**
  If there is someone you admire who has overcome obstacles in the past and so will be able to relate to your own challenges they could be a useful mentor. A mentor is someone with whom you can talk things over and who can offer you some thoughts and guidance. A mentor won't tell you what to do, but will help to ensure that you think things through and might suggest ways of tackling issues which you haven't thought of. There are professional mentors out there but they will charge you for their services; it is better to ask people you know or people who are recommended to you. As long as they have sufficient time, most people will be pleased to give you some guidance

When people help you it's important to show your gratitude. You'd be surprised at how many people don't say thank you when someone has done them a favour. Saying thank you marks you out as a likeable person and it affirms your relationship with people.

When I met a student on an internship we got

talking about what she was doing. The next day she asked to connect with me on LinkedIn with an accompanying note to say she had appreciated our talk.

It's important to show your gratitude

The fact that she said thank you made her stick in my mind. One day I might just remember her if an opportunity arises at my company, and I'll be more inclined to help her with advice if she asks because I know she will be grateful. The thing about networking is that you may not need specific help straight away but one day, when you do, you will have a better chance of knowing someone who can give that help.

Finally, be reciprocal. Offer your help to people too. What goes around comes around.

What I currently do has no relevance

I once helped to run a training course for veterans who had served in the armed forces and who had suffered badly from post-traumatic stress disorder. Many of them were at an all-time low but all of them were desperate to take back control of their lives. Finding meaningful employment was critical to this. The training involved helping them to write CVs and to practise interview skills. One man was almost in tears when he said to me, 'I don't know what to put on my CV. I really want to build railways but I have no experience'. I asked him what he had done in the army and what he felt he was good at. He replied, 'All I can do is clean a gun and fit it together. What use is that?' I explained that he had some very relevant transferrable skills:

- If you know how to put together the component parts of a gun you understand mechanisms and have engineering and technical ability. Building railways requires the same skills, just with bigger components

- If you work with guns you pay attention to detail. If you are not accurate, precise and careful then the gun will not function and may be dangerous. On a railway, if the parts don't fit together perfectly, trains won't be able to run, so attention to detail, accuracy and precision are key

- When you are in charge of a gun, you have people's lives in your hands and you carry responsibility and accountability for that. Building a railway requires the same level of responsibility and accountability

- In the army you learn to work as a team and your colleagues rely on you. When building a railway you work with a team in exactly the same way

My trainee was able to look at his CV with a new confidence – the possibility of him being able to change career suddenly became more plausible.

This is the power of transferrable skills. All jobs require many of the same basic skills and these usually form a major part of the requirements. The most common transferrable skills are:

- **Good communication**

    Are you good at writing succinct content for reports or web pages? Can you understand complex issues and explain them clearly? Are you good at talking to people and putting them at their ease? Are you good at presenting? Are you a good listener? Can you negotiate, persuade or influence people in a nice way? Are you good on the telephone?

- **Good people skills**

    Are you a good team member? Are you a motivational and supportive people manager? Do you nurture effective relationships with customers or suppliers? Are you good at managing conflict? Do you deal well with members of the public?

- **Good organisation**
  Are you well organised? Can you cope with lots of tasks at once? Can you prioritise? Are you flexible? Can you move quickly from one thing to another if you need to? Do you keep calm in a crisis? Are you good at planning?

Think about the job you do now and the job you'd like to have. How many of the above skills or other skills do you currently have? List them, write down concrete examples of times when you have demonstrated them and ideas on how you could use them in your dream position. Use this information to demonstrate your suitability for the role when you make your job application or when you are asked about relevant skills in an interview.

I have been out of the workplace for too long

Even if you have had a career break or stayed at home to look after a family, you will have transferrable skills (see the previous chapter for more on these). Think about your experiences: do you help at a school, belong to a parents' association, have a hobby, organise charity events, volunteer or juggle and organise family commitments? Do you help with a scouts group or children's sports team? All of these take organisation, people skills, leadership, communication, flexibility, prioritisation and teamwork.

Think about activities you have participated in and your role in them, or situations where you have had to demonstrate tenacity or perseverance. For example, was there a time you had to stand up for your rights in a shop because of faulty goods and put forward your reasons in a persuasive way? Have you organised a big family holiday which involved complicated travel arrangements involving multiple kinds of transport and timetables? You may have also demonstrated good communication skills speaking to tourist offices, where English might not have been their first language, to confirm bookings.

> You will have transferrable skills

We develop transferrable skills in all aspects of our lives. It doesn't matter what you've been doing over the past few years you will definitely have some, and some of these will be needed in your dream role. The key is to prepare your list of examples (as mentioned in the previous chapter) so that you have a reminder of what you can offer an employer.

The Application

I don't have any time to complete the application

Job applications do take time, especially if you want yours to get noticed. The job market is competitive so it's important to spend time on an application in order to stand out from the crowd. Remember that getting the job will enhance your life: you will be doing something you love and you will have a lifestyle you enjoy. You might also be earning more money or enjoying any number of other benefits depending on the role and company. Keep that vision in your mind when thinking about completing that application.

> Remember that getting the job will enhance your life

Time is a very important commodity and we set aside time for all sorts of things which make us happy (time with loved ones, holidays, reading a good book). If you change your mindset and see time spent on job applications as an investment in your happiness, then you'll find it easier to make it a priority – it will become one of those things which makes you happy and therefore it will take on new significance and importance.

For more on making time in a busy life, see "I'm too busy in my current job to look for another one".

Applying for jobs is tedious

Applying for jobs can be laborious if you are going to do it well. It's not just a matter of dashing off a generic letter and keeping your fingers crossed. Companies get hundreds of applications for every job they advertise so you need to make yours stand out.

If you don't feel motivated to apply for a role, it might not be your dream job at all! So ask yourself these questions:

- Am I really interested in this company's products and services? Would I use them myself?
- Has this company got a good reputation? Would I be proud to work for them?
- Does this position meet all my dream job criteria?
- Would I be really excited if I got this role?
- Would I feel really upset in two weeks' time if I hadn't applied and missed the deadline?

If the answers to the above are all yes then the application process should be exciting, not boring! You should feel be motivated to put your best into your application as this is your first opportunity to get noticed.

If your answers to the above questions are no, then you *are* likely to find the application process tedious as it doesn't sound like the right application for you.

I don't know how to write a CV

Putting together a CV might seem daunting but all CVs have a standard basic structure. A CV should have the following sections:

- Your name and contact information
- A personal statement or short summary of who you are
- Work history or experience in chronological order, starting with your current position
- Relevant skills to the job in question
- Other achievements and interests
- Contacts for references

Presentation is very important so take the time to make your CV clear, concise and easy to read, and check it carefully for spelling mistakes and typos – it helps to have someone else read it through too.

When you have your basic CV you can then tailor it for specific jobs. It is not enough to have one CV which you use for everything.

All the information you need to use to tailor your CV is in the job description so read it carefully to make sure you have understood exactly what the employer is asking for. Even if you are applying for similar jobs you still need to ensure your CV is adapted to the company to which you are applying. All companies are different – they all have different cultures, values and ways of doing things. The clues will be in what is emphasised in the job description. Then you can be sure you include all the right things on your CV.

> It is not enough to have one CV which you use for everything

Your personal statement needs to sum up your skills and experience and persuade the recruiter to read on. It should be only four or five lines long, be succinct and pertinent to the job. For example:

I am an award-winning sales assistant with eight years' experience of styling customers, receiving positive reviews and consistently exceeding my monthly sales targets. I have designed window displays resulting in increasing footfall and augmenting handbag sales and am now looking for my next role in window display where I can use my skills and make an impact on sales targets.

Use positive and assertive language. For example, rather than say 'I *had to* carry out a survey', write 'I *devised* and *prepared* a survey'. Instead of using passive words, try to use active words. These active words show that you are a person who has initiative and takes action. Some useful assertive verbs are:

Developed	Created	Evaluated
Assessed	Co-ordinated	Researched
Arranged	Recommended	Analysed
Advised	Taught	Explained
Persuaded	Organised	Led
Managed		

For the rest of your CV highlight all the aspects of the job which you are most suited to and give examples to demonstrate this. Use *all* of your experience, not just examples from your current job. Think back to what you have done in the past and what you do outside of work. Look at the areas where you feel you have less experience and see if you have any transferrable skills.

For example, if a job requires experience of problem

solving and you have experience of dealing with customer product complaints then you can link these: you have experience of understanding the customer's issue, liaising with the manufacturer and the quality control team, sourcing a suitable replacement, keeping the customer informed, writing appropriate emails or letters and checking that everyone is satisfied with the outcome. Your CV might therefore state that you 'have good experience of dealing with a wide range of customer problems from faulty goods to bad service and are responsible for investigating these and offering solutions'. If you have statistics to back this up you could also say you 'have a track record of resolving problems satisfactorily demonstrated by a consistent customer satisfaction score of 99%'. Your statements shows that not only have you had relevant experience but that you are good at it.

Is there anything you have done which makes you stand out from the crowd? This might be something unusual you have done outside of work, a foreign language ability, a challenging event you have organised, a place visited that required you to use your initiative to get there or an experience which has required you to be extra resilient, patient, calm or resourceful. For examples of your interests don't use passive things like reading or watching films but use examples which show off skills such as leading a local football team, sitting on a committee, or organising charity events.

These types of examples will show that you can operate in challenging circumstances. They also demonstrate that you have a broad range of experiences and an enthusiastic and positive outlook on life.

Ensure that you include anything you have done voluntarily to upskill yourself. Employers are very impressed when people try to help themselves and it shows that you are truly interested in the role.

Remember that a CV is not the story of your life and so you don't need to list every single activity and task you have ever done. What is important is to give the recruiter the sense that you have had the responsibility, experience and achievements that they are looking for, are skilled and qualified to do this role and that you stand out more than the other applicants in this respect. You have to do this succinctly so try to keep your CV to two pages as recruiters don't have time to read more when they have hundreds of applicants.

One final point – *never* lie on your CV. You will be found out either during the interview or when they take references or do background checks. It is not worth it. Don't make up qualifications or experience you don't have. You will ruin all future trust in you and you'll have wasted all the time and effort you've put in so far.

I don't know how to write a covering letter

Your covering letter or email is your opportunity to market yourself and to persuade the recruiter to select you for interview.

Here are some tips:

- Keep it fairly short – you don't want to repeat everything that is in your CV
- Address it to an actual person. If there is no name in the advert consider contacting the company and asking for a name
- Be clear in the heading and first line what job you are applying for (state job title and any reference) and where you saw it advertised
- Explain why you are applying for this role, why you feel you are suitable and why the company excites you

An example might be:

Dear Ms Smith

Re: Application reference 1224 for Assistant Window Display Designer

I am writing to apply for the above role, advertised in the Daily Echo on Tuesday 3rd February.

For the last three years I have been working for Jones' department store as a sales assistant in the women's wear department where I am responsible for ensuring the stock is well presented and for serving customers. In particular, I help customers to select clothes and outfits for special occasions and have a reputation for enhancing them with unusual and eye-catching accessories. I have had consistently positive customer feedback during this time.

My dream role is to be responsible for window dressing and to use my creative skills to help attract customers. To this end, over the last eighteen months I have volunteered to assist our window dresser in my own time. I have gained a good understanding of how to design attractive and unusual window displays to draw in customers and, when I was given the opportunity to design the Christmas handbag display, sales of handbags increased by 15% and many people complimented me on the display, including the store manager. I was named Employee of the Month in December.

The position of assistant window display designer at your store really excites me. Your store has a renowned reputation for its creativity and the quality of its goods. I understand that you will shortly be introducing a new range of jewellery and accessories and I would love to use my proven skills and experience to put together attractive and enticing window displays to promote these.

I am a quick learner and would be prepared to undertake any training you offer to enable me to give my very best to this role.

I would be delighted to talk to you further about my experience and what I can offer and hope that I will be given the opportunity to do so at an interview.

I enclose my CV and can provide you with references about my work. I am also able to share with you photographs of the window displays I have assisted with or designed.

I look forward to hearing from you.

Check everything more than once. Sleep on your application and then read it again with fresh eyes before you post it. Have you covered all the points the job application stated were important? Have you missed out a vital example of your experience? Do you feel your letter sells you in the best possible way? Sometimes it helps to read what you have written out loud – does it flow well? Are your sentences so long you run out of breath reading them? If so, add punctuation or split out your points. Have you checked your spelling and grammar? Sometimes when you are very close to something you can't see the wood for the trees so ask someone else to read the letter and give feedback. .

Taking time to double and triple check your application is well worth it. You want to give yourself the best possible chance of being invited for interview.

I'll do it tomorrow

Lots of tomorrows will come and go while you are saying this! It is easy to put things off and fill your day with other 'stuff' but here is some advice on how to organise yourself so that you make a start and stop delaying:

When are you at your best? For some people it is first thing in the morning, for others it's later in the day.

The most important thing is to diarise some time at your best time of the day. You don't have to do everything in one go, you could set aside two hours as a starting point. Organise a time when you won't be disturbed so that you can focus. Don't feel tempted to switch on the TV or radio, and make sure you are comfortable and have a drink or snack to hand so that you don't have to break off and go searching for one.

> Be clear on what you want or need to achieve

Be clear on what you want or need to achieve first – for instance getting to know some key facts about the company you want to work for or setting out all your transferrable skills and how these might be used in the job for which you are applying.

Setting aside a specific length of time for a specific task means you will have accomplished something at the end of two hours and this will feel like a success. If you try to do everything at once you're unlikely to finish it and will then feel disappointed in yourself.

Promise yourself that at the end of the two hours you will do something completely different – go for a walk, meet a friend, go shopping or just sit and read.

Then schedule your next two hour slot and decide how you are going to use it. This way you will start to tick off all the tasks on your action plan.

The Interview

I don't know what to wear

What you wear and how you present yourself will determine the interviewer's first impression of you. It is therefore important to get it right.

These days many offices are more relaxed in their dress code and some industries are now completely dress-down – I have visited fin-tech companies where the standard dress is jeans. However, if you are going for an interview I recommend you err on the side of caution and go business smart. For example, even if you know everyone normally wears jeans in the office, you might want to consider upgrading to trousers and a jacket. If you are visiting a large corporate, suits or smart business clothes are the safest option. It is always better to arrive too dressed up than too dressed down.

Plan what you are going to wear a few days beforehand. Try things on. Make sure what you plan to wear is comfortable – you don't want to be constantly adjusting your clothes or find that you are not at ease in them at the interview. Having your outfit planned and ready on the day will help you feel more relaxed and in control.

Wearing the right clothes and feeling comfortable in them will make you feel more confident – you look the part, you feel relaxed, now all you have to focus on are the questions.

I get tongue-tied and don't know what to say

When you are asked a question it is tempting to rush in with your answer because even a few seconds of slience can feel like an eternity. However, in reality every interviewer will expect a small pause while you consider your answer. In fact if you rush in too quickly the interviewer will wonder if you have actually considered their question carefully enough. At the same time you don't want to stretch it out to the point that there is an embarrassing silence.

You need to be able to answer the questions factually and succinctly. You don't want to find yourself waffling and you need to be able to give facts and examples from your career or experience that answer the questions as relevantly as possible.

This is where good preparation is key. Before you go for the interview think of all the questions you may be asked. Most interviewers will explore similar areas and ask for examples of where you have demonstrated particular skills. Write down all the questions you think you may be asked and then write down two or three relevant examples you could refer to in your answers. Don't worry if you have to call on experience outside your current job. For example if you sit on a local committee and have to organise the agenda and meetings or if you coach a local sports team where you have to encourage people to work together. They are all good examples. You might find that the experience you gained on a certain project helps you to answer several questions – for example, it might show good organisation, how you managed people with conflicting interests and your calmness under pressure. It is fine to draw on one experience to illustrate two points but try to have several examples to demonstrate you have done something more than once.

> Think of all the questions you may be asked

If the person you meet is a good interviewer they will ask you one question at a time. However less experienced or impatient interviewers might ask several questions at once! Take a moment to sort them out in your mind. Breathe slowly and repeat the questions in your head – this way you will remember them. I can remember one important interview where I was asked to 'give a summary of my career history, what I was most proud of achieving and what were the most significant takeaways I had learned from each job'. Answering those questions all at once when you have a career spanning thirty years is quite a challenge and I definitely needed a few moments to consider which were the most important things I had to say.

Occasionally you may be asked an unexpected question. Don't panic. It is absolutely fine to ask if you can have a moment to think about what you have been asked. This way you can reflect for a moment and give a measured response. It is also fine to say that you may not have had direct experience but give the closest example you can think of. For example, you may not have had direct experience of dealing with an angry customer in a shop but you might have had experience of dealing with someone else who was upset or angry in a different environment. The interviewer will mainly be interested in how you diffused or dealt with the situation, not where it took place.

> It is absolutely fine to ask if you can have a moment to think

We can all get tongue-tied or flustered sometimes but if you think about the questions you may be asked beforehand and plan what you would like to say it will help you to feel more in control and much more relaxed.

If you need more advice in this area, have a look at Paul Falcone's book, 96 Great Interview Questions to Ask Before You Hire.[12] It sets out questions for interviewers to ask and explains why they ask them and the type of answers they are looking for.

I get so nervous

Everyone feels a bit nervous when going for an interview – it's completely normal. In fact, having a few nerves is usually a good thing as it helps us to focus our minds and concentrate. I take part in amateur dramatics and I am always terrified that I will forget my first line when I go on stage. I can't understand anyone who doesn't have a few nerves in those sorts of situations – it's not normal! However, while having a few nerves is fine, it is a good idea to minimise them as far as possible.

Here's how you do that:

- **Prepare well**

    If you have prepared what you want to say in response to the more standard questions it will give you one less thing to be nervous about (see more

---

12 Paul Falcone, 96 Great Interview Questions to Ask Before You Hire, Amacom, 2018

on this in the previous chapter)

- **Practise interviews with a friend**
  Get them to ask you all sorts of questions in different ways. It is one thing to rehearse answers in your head but it is quite different when you say those answers out loud. From my experience as an actor in an amateur fringe theatre group I know it is easy to think you have learnt your words for a part when you are saying them in your head but as soon as you put the script down and say those words out loud it is far more difficult. The more the cast say the words out loud the better we become. It is just the same with interviews – you will get better at being succinct and articulate as you practise and then when you are next asked a question your reply will be natural. Your friends will also be able to critique you and suggest other ways of saying things

- **Remember that most interviewers are on your side**
  The fact that you have been invited to interview means that the interviewer is interested in you. There will be many applicants who didn't get through the first selection stage and actually getting to meet someone and talk to them in person is a big achievement. The interviewer wants to fill their

job so is going to give you every opportunity to demonstrate that you are the right person for it. They will also make an effort to put you at your ease so that you can perform well

- **Sit in a good position**
  If you have a choice of seat, choose one where you can see the interviewer comfortably and avoid sitting where the sun is in your eyes or where you are at an awkward angle. Get into a comfortable position so that you don't have to shuffle about. Place your hands in your lap and don't fold your arms. Folding your arms may be comfortable and may stop you fidgeting but it can come across as aggressive or defensive, when you should be trying to appear open and friendly

- **Relax your breathing**
  If you are nervous your voice can sound strained and you should obviously be aiming to sound relaxed and confident. So take a calm breath before speaking and try not to make your sentences so long that you run out of breath! Remember, the interviewer is genuinely interested in what you have to say. You have practised your answers and you know you have the ability to do this job

- **Look the interviewer in the eye**
  If you look down or away then again this shows a lack of confidence. When you speak to people you feel comfortable with you look them in the eye so do the same here, and don't be afraid to smile. It shows interest, engagement, confidence and conviction in what you are saying

Throughout the interview try to bear in mind that you have come to discuss your dream job so this should be an interesting and exciting experience, not something to be endured!

I don't know how to reply when they ask if I have anything else to add

This is your opportunity to say anything important that you might not have had a chance to say so far. For example, if there is something you have done in the past which would really add weight to how well suited you are for the job then say it now. For example, you could say, 'We discussed the importance of customer service in this role and one example I didn't give you was… I just wanted to add that as I know how vital this is'.

If you haven't got anything else to add then use this as a chance to simply reiterate how interested you are in the role.

I don't know what to say when they ask if I have any questions

This is your chance to ask something which shows you are interested in the position and the company and it's best if you plan some questions before the interview.

Some good questions could be:

- Asking about the key focus of the role in the coming year: 'It would be really interesting to know what the big priority issues are for this role in the next twelve months'. This shows you are interested in prioritising and focusing on what is most important

- Asking about potential colleagues: 'Who are the most influential people I would work with and what do they consider the most important part of my role?'

- Asking about the strategy of the company: 'What is the main strategic focus of the company over the next one to three years and how do you see this position contributing?' or 'I read that the company is expanding into a new product area – will this position be involved with that?' This demonstrates that you take an interest in things outside of your own job

- Exploring opportunities to get involved in other areas: for instance you could ask about the company's corporate social responsibility policy and whether there are opportunities to help or give back to their chosen charities or the community in which you would be working

If you really can't think of anything then try this: 'I would be really interested to hear your story and how you find working here', or 'I am just starting out in my career but one day I would love to have a similar position to you – how have you achieved your position?'

Avoid any questions which assume that you have got the job! Don't ask about trivia like where you might be sitting and avoid talking about money at this stage too. There is plenty of time to discuss money if you get offered the job!

Finally, there is nothing wrong with saying 'We have really covered a lot in the interview and you answered my questions as we went along so I don't have anything else to ask at the moment, thank you'.

I find it hard to sell myself

Few people find it easy to be a salesperson for their own skills. Unfortunately you have to be one in an interview.

A good way to build up your confidence in this area is to talk to other people and ask them how they would sell you! Choose people you trust and whose opinion you respect. Be brave too though – if you choose people with whom you get on all the time then they are bound to give you a glowing review. If you ask those people you respect but with whom you may have a more difficult relationship you will get useful honest feedback about what they think about working with you. Ask all of these people to tell you about your strengths and to give examples about when they have seen you demonstrate these.

You also need to be prepared to be asked about your weaknesses – and we all have some! You may already know what you are less good at but you can also talk these over with trusted friends and colleagues. You may find that other people don't think they are weaknesses at all! The important thing is to pick the weaknesses you mention in interview carefully; don't choose something which would be critical to the role! Try also to mention something where you can demonstrate you have made a conscious effort to improve. For example, you may say that you find it hard to say no and therefore can take on too much work as you really like to help all of your customers and this can lead to you having to stay late in order not to miss deadlines. You can then go on to say that you are addressing this by setting more realistic timeframes for getting back to people and allowing for some contingency so you can set and meet customer expectations and maintain your high standards of service.

Honest and constructive feedback is invaluable. There is nothing more powerful than saying at an interview that you believe that you are good at something, that you asked people to give you feedback and they confirmed it and gave examples. Showing that you genuinely seek feedback and openly discuss how you can improve with people is something also worth showing off.

In summary, the more you have analysed your skills, experience, strengths and weaknesses before the interview, the better you will be able to talk about them. This way it won't feel so much like a sales pitch.

Finances

I can't afford to retrain

Depending on the training you need to do, at this moment the cost might well appear to be prohibitive.

But you do have options:

- **Saving**

  You might want to review the suggestions for saving money in the next chapter with a view to making savings for a period of time to build up a training fund. Alternatively could you temporarily take on an additional evening or weekend job to earn extra money to build your fund?

- **Taking out a loan**

  You may want to consider this, particularly if your dream job is well-paid and there are plenty of opportunities once you are qualified. However, make sure you fully understand the repayment and interest terms and carefully consider whether you can really afford it – a loan could be a good option but it could also exacerbate financial worries if you aren't confident that you can afford the repayments. If a bank loan is too daunting would a member of your family be willing to help you? With family, make sure you fully understand their expectations regarding repayment so that it doesn't cause problems between you

- **Sponsorship**
  Would it be possible to get some kind of sponsorship? Some companies may do this on the condition you stay with them for a certain period of time after qualifying and the qualification is relevant to what you are doing as well. Speak to your manager or human resources department

If your dream role is likely to be a well-paid one it could well be worth investing in your qualification now, but do be realistic about this.

My dream job won't pay enough

There is no denying that money is important in our lives – we have rent or a mortgage and bills to pay, families to support and multiple other obligations. Money concerns can't be dismissed lightly. In fact, it is a well-known fact that money worries are one of the biggest causes of stress and so it doesn't matter how much you might want a career change, the reality of money has to be taken into consideration.

If your dream role pays less than your current job it's worth doing a detailed budget review.

Have a good look at your day-to-day outgoings – are there any areas where you could make savings? You could shop around for better deals on regular bills such as fuel and broadband and consider opting for cheaper brands of clothing, food, homewares, etc.

Are there any luxuries which you enjoy now which you'd be willing to reduce or cut out to save money and make doing your dream job more viable? If you regularly buy coffee on the way to your current job every morning, estimate how much you might save if you made it in the office instead. How much could you save if you took your own lunch into work? Saving just one pound every working day adds up to two hundred and sixty pounds a year.

> It's worth doing a detailed budget review

List all of the non-essential things you spend money on. Highlight those you really don't want to give up. See if you can think of any alternatives.

Do you really need to buy so many clothes? And can you find free activities at the weekend such as walking and visiting museums and art galleries? Going to a local theatre rather than an expensive high-profile show or early-bird showings at cinemas could help too.

This cutting down may only have to be temporary until you get established in your new role but if it needs to be a longer term change, think about ways in which you might be able to increase income. Would it be possible for you to combine two jobs, spending part of the week in your current work and part of the week in your ideal job? Or is your dream job something you could do at weekends? Work such as construction, animal care, hospitality all require people to work weekends. This way you'd earn more than making the move full-time and you could assess how you get on with your finances before you transition fully. See more about this in "Is it OK to compromise?"

Also don't forget to check the employee benefits which prospective new companies might offer. Many employers organise discounts with certain retailers for their employees, which means you might enjoy regular savings in food, clothing white good and even things like travel insurance. All these savings would help and don't underestimate how small savings can add up. [13]

Other benefits may be available too – for instance if you need glasses to look at a computer screen there

---

13 *For more ideas on saving money see Jo Thresher's "What's Your Excuse for not Being Better With Money?" WYE Publishing, 2016*

is usually a contribution towards the cost, and a new employer's pension package may be more generous than your current one.

When you are assessing the financial viability of your transition, consider the potential lifestyle change too. I always say that when you choose to work for a company you are also choosing a lifestyle. Some jobs demand long hours, some lots of travel, some a more flexible working pattern. Your dream job will come with its own lifestyle and you need to assess its impact on your life.

> Perhaps the reduction in income is worth it

If your ideal job will mean a more relaxed lifestyle, perhaps the reduction in income is worth it. For example, is it better to enjoy going to work each day and cook at home in the evenings or to spend five days a week unhappy in your role but eat out in restaurants? You spend a vast amount of time working and if you love what you do and get satisfaction from it then cutting back in other areas of your life may be worth it.

Changing your job and doing something you love can bring about a change of priorities. I have a friend who used to have a very stressful career and spent a lot of money going on long-haul holidays to compensate. She changed career and became self-employed. Now she feels she doesn't need such expensive breaks from her job as she enjoys her work and has an improved quality of life. Her holidays these days are self-catering in the UK, but she enjoys them just as much. She also no longer needs to spend money on ready meals or takeaways because she now has time to cook, she no longer needs to buy expensive suits to impress in the boardroom and she no longer needs to spend so much on commuting and taxis home after working late into the evenings.

Sometimes happiness can be more valuable than having lots of money.

Getting the Job

I'm worried about what other people might think of me

You should be immensely proud if you have succeeded in getting the job of your dreams. Most people will be delighted for you. Even if you have radically changed direction or given up a high-powered and highly-paid job to do something less well-paid it shouldn't matter to other people. The fact that you are doing what you have always wanted to do and your enthusiasm for your new work will generally impress and inspire others.

Occasionally though you might be faced with people who don't think like you and it is a sad fact that our status in society is often defined by the job we do. When

> Be confident about your choice. It is making you happy

we meet new people often the first thing we are asked is what we do for a living. If you are worried about how your answer may be received by someone you're meeting for the first time, you can minimise the chance of any negative reactions by prefixing your reply with

'I am doing something I always wanted to do…' Be confident about your choice. It is making you happy.

If family or friends disapprove of your choice it can be disappointing, as these are often the people we wish to impress most and who we most want to be proud of us. But again, this is your choice, not theirs and if you are happy and able to support yourself financially there's no reason for them to disapprove.

Remember, you are your own person. You cannot live someone else's life for them and they cannot live their life through you. Life is short and you should therefore do all you can to be happy. The people who care about you should understand that and support you in your career choice and if they don't it may be more to do with how they feel about themselves than how they feel about you.

It's actually impossible to change the way other people think – you can only change how you react to them – so in this case be proud of what you have achieved and your new happy lifestyle. You're doing it for you.

Is it OK to compromise?

Sometimes it is OK to compromise and in fact in some cases there are good reasons to do so.

If you're concerned that a 'big bang' approach to a career change might be too daunting or not financially viable you could combine your dream job with something which gives you some security and stability.

A contact of mine had always wanted to set up a coaching business, but was aware that coaching was unlikely to pay anything like what she was currently earning in her role as director of consultancy for an IT company. She had a large mortgage and a comfortable lifestyle and although she was willing to cut back in some areas, she wasn't quite ready to downsize her home! So she left her full-time job, but sought out part-time contract work with a similar company to cover her mortgage and basic living costs, and then trained as a coach. This enabled her to do what she had always wanted to do, but with little financial risk. She was able to do this because she had built up a good reputation in the IT industry and had nurtured a network of useful contacts – see "If my current job could be improved it would be my dream role" for more on building a reputation and "I don't know the right people" for more on networks.

At fourteen I really, *really* wanted to be an actress. But as I got older I understood that this is a risky business and I wanted financial security so I started down a more traditional career route. In fact this was not a bad move. Over the years, I have come to learn both what I like doing and what I am good at and I get a lot of satisfaction from the work I do: solving business problems, setting policy, presenting at seminars and supporting employees. I seek out projects which allow me to be creative and have a lot of fun doing them. But the actress in me hasn't entirely died – it comes out when I am invited to speak at events and for the past twenty-two years I have acted and directed with a local amateur fringe theatre group. It is a happy compromise for me, which combines security with doing what I love.

So yes, it is entirely OK to compromise, as long as you are doing it for the right reasons.

And finally, this also applies if you are struggling to secure the role you want on a full-time basis. Look for ways of combining involvement in your dream activity with what you do currently, even if it's on a voluntary basis. At the very least you're doing it some of the time and at best it could lead to bigger, better opportunities in the future.

Some Final Thoughts

As I said at the beginning of this book, my personal mantra is to follow your dreams. To do that you will need to be determined, patient at times and resilient.

Treat your quest for your dream job as a project. Be organised, break down what you need to do into manageable tasks and tackle them one at a time.

It won't always be easy but you should persevere and don't get discouraged. Try your best – if you do that, then you can do no more. The most important thing is to have no regrets.

To set you on your way, here are a few important reminders:

Dream jobs don't always have a job title – they are sometimes about doing more of the things you enjoy in your current role. Therefore it is worth talking to your manager or human resources department before you consider moving on.

If you know what your dream job is but need some additional skills or experience then volunteer to get involved in projects where you can develop these skills.

Remember that you will definitely have some transferrable skills that apply to your dream job. Don't underestimate these.

There are lots of ways of getting skills and qualifications so it may not be as daunting as you think. Talk to your friends and colleagues as they may have contacts who can help you.

If you can't get experience then don't be afraid of creating your own!

When you applying for a job application give it the appropriate amount of attention – this is an investment in your future. Ensure that your CV is tailored to the role for which you are applying. Use your covering letter to highlight the reasons why you are interested in this role and the skills and experience you can bring to the job. Check and re-check your application before sending it.

If you get an interview you should be proud of yourself. Most jobs get hundreds of applicants and if you have been selected for further discussion then you have stood out from the crowd. Getting a foot in the door and the opportunity to meet a prospective employer face to face is a big achievement and it's your chance to sell yourself and shine. Prepare well for your interview to ensure you give your absolute best performance.

Finally, remember that employers put out a 'wish list' when they advertise jobs so don't feel you have to tick every box – they often have a much shorter list of what is essential, and you can learn in the job. Enthusiasm, passion and reliability count for a lot.

I hope you now feel excited about pursuing your dream job. Enjoy the application process, enjoy learning about potential new employers, enjoy learning new skills and enjoy the feeling of working towards your dream.

If you need inspiration, here are some thoughts from Roz Savage who left her role as a management consultant in her thirties to become the first woman to row across the three major oceans. She says:

> 'First, I realised that my job, although it paid me well, was not making me happy. One day, I sat down and wrote two versions of my own obituary: the one I wanted to have, and the one I was heading for if I carried on my current path. My job was not taking me the way that I wanted to go. It was, in fact, taking me in the opposite direction, toward a life of tedium and obligation rather than one of freedom and fulfillment'[14]

I think this illustrates just how important it is to strive for what you really want to do so you have no regrets in the future.

The job market is in an interesting state of transition due to the impact of technology and globalisation. This means that if you are curious and flexible, willing to learn and apply yourself, the world job market is open to you. Employers want people who are eager to learn, can demonstrate new skills and can bring different and diverse thoughts and views to the table. If ever there

---

14   https://www.rozsavage.com/about/rozs-story

was a time to get excited about changing career and trying to get that dream job, it is now.

While there is no doubt that you do need to be prepared to put time, effort and hard work into getting your dream job, the reward of doing something exciting, rewarding and enjoyable *will* be worth it. Don't end up thinking 'if only'. Be courageous.

I wish you every success.

Acknowledgements

I would not have written this book nor had the confidence to follow my own dreams without my wonderful mum and dad, Mary and Norman Lemon, who have always encouraged and supported me in what I've wanted to do. A huge thank you and so much love to them – you have been the best parents as well as my special friends.

I also want to say thank you to my two fantastic children, John and Jane. They are just starting out on their adult lives and careers and I have had many enriching conversations with them about how the world of work is changing and their own career aspirations. Thank you both for sharing your thoughts with me and supporting me as I wrote! I am immensely proud of you both – you are amazing, kind young people with great moral and work ethics. I hope you will both follow your dreams. Please know that I will always be there for you and that I love you to the moon and back and more! This book is dedicated to you both.

When undergoing any project it makes such a difference to be surrounded and supported by friends, family and colleagues so I really want to acknowledge and thank the following people: my lovely, patient and very understanding editor and publisher Joanne Henson, my Hays colleagues Paul Venables and Doug Evans who have actively encouraged and supported me in writing this book, my friend and associate Daniel Shakhani who first introduced me to Joanne through his amazing network and who has taken an active interest in my book's progression, my husband Tony Burton and all my friends who have been so kind in their interest and words of encouragement. A big thank you to you all.

About the Author

Rosemary Lemon is Group Head of Reward for Hays plc and has interviewed and recruited candidates for a wide range of roles in a number of different industries (recruitment, energy, shipping and logistics, luxury retail and financial services).

She has been involved in many interesting government and charity projects and initiatives and in 2018 she was awarded the Reward & Employee Benefits Association's Vanguard Award for her work throughout her career promoting and recognising the importance of employee wellbeing.

She is a member of the government's Money Advice Service steering committee, working to increase the financial capability of working people across the UK and she is a member of the Remuneration Committee for the London Metropolitan University.

Over the course of her career, she has worked with employees at all levels, from young people just starting out on their careers to the most senior board members. Her personal mantra is that jobs are what you make them and that work is such a large part of your life it is important you follow your dreams.

Index

A
Age	36, 41
Application	**69**

C
Can't afford to retrain	93
Clothing	81
Compromise	100
Covering letter	76
Cullen, Amanda	29
Current job	
could be improved	27
has no relevance	63
Too busy with to look for a new one	23
CV	71
Don't know how to write	71

D
Don't have	
the right experience	51
the right qualifications	56
the right skills	54
Don't know	
how to reply to questions	88
how to write a covering letter	76
how to write a CV	71
the right people	59
what my dream job would be	23
what to ask	89
what to say	82, 88, 89
what to wear	81
where to look for vacancies	30

E
Experience	51
Experience, don't have the right	51

F
Failure, frightened of	35
Falcone, Paul	85
Fears	**35**
Finances	**93**
Frightened of failure	35

G
Getting the Job	**99**

H
Headhunters	**33**

I
Interview **81**
Interview questions 88, 89

J
Job title 25

L
Landau-Pope, Juliet 24
LinkedIn 59

M
Mentors 62
Money 93

N
Nerves 85
Nervous, I get 85
Networking 32, 52, 59

O
Other people, worried about
what they will think 99

P
Past experiences 45
Pay, my dream job won't
enough 94
People
Don't know the right 59
Worried about what
they will think 99

Q
Qualifications 56
Qualifications, don't have
the right 56

R
Recruitment agencies 30
Reputation 27
Retrain, can't afford to 93
Risky, it's too 43

S
Savage, Roz 107
Selling yourself 91
Skills 54
Don't have the right 54
Transferrable 64, 67
Skills and Qualifications **51**

T
Tedious, applying for jobs is 70
Thresher, Jo 96
Time, I don't have any to
complete the application 69
Tomorrow, I'll do it 79
Tongue-tied, I get and don't
know what to say 82
Too old 36
Too risky 43
Too young 41
Training 54
Transferable skills 64, 67
Tried it before and didn't
succeed 45

V
Vacancies 30

W

Workplace, have been out
for too long 66
Worried about what other
people might think 99

Also in this series

What's Your Excuse for not Being More Productive?

Juliet Landau-Pope
Overcome your excuses, stop procrastinating, get things done

Do you struggle to organise your time? Do you spend too much time planning and not enough time doing? Or are you simply unable to get started with things? Then this is the book for you.

Professional organiser Juliet-Landau Pope takes a look at all of the things you might be telling yourself to explain why you're not being as productive as you'd like, and offers practical advice, ideas and inspiration to help you move forward.

Don't know where to start? Don't have the time? Or do you simply feel overwhelmed? This supportive and motivational book will help you to tackle all of those beliefs and many more so that you can use your time more effectively in order to *get things done*.

Paperback – ISBN 978-0-9956052-2-0
e-book – ISBN 978-0-9956052-3-7

Also in this series

What's Your Excuse for not Overcoming Stress?

Kelly Swingler
Overcome your excuses for less stress and more control, calm and resilience

Do you struggle with stress in your life? Do you feel out of control, overwhelmed, under pressure or unable to relax?

In this supportive and motivational book Kelly Swingler takes a look at all of the reasons why you may be tolerating stress in your life. She explains how you can take action to reduce it and offers practical strategies, simple tips, guidance and inspiration to help you bring about positive change.

Learn how to switch off from the things you can't change and take control of those you can, to feel calmer, happier and more positive about yourself and your life.

Paperback – ISBN 978-0-9933388-6-8
e-book – ISBN 978-0-9933388-7-5

Also in this series

What's Your Excuse for not Being Better With Money?

Jo Thresher
Overcome your excuses and get to grips with your personal finances

Do you wish you could be savvier with money but find it too daunting? Do you wish you were more in control of your finances but find yourself avoiding taking action? Then this is the book for you.

Personal finance expert Jo Thresher takes a look at all of the reasons you might give for not getting to grips with your money, and offers advice, ideas and inspiration to help you change that.

No time to get organised? Scared to look at your bank statement? Think you're a shopaholic? Not money minded? Overcome all of these excuses and many more. Improve your relationship with your cash and feel more secure, more relaxed and more in control.

Paperback – ISBN 978-0-9956052-0-6
e-book – ISBN 978-0-9956052-1-3

Also in this series

What's Your Excuse for not Loving Your Job?

Amanda Cullen
Overcome your excuses and change the way you feel about your work

Do you have a job which you're not enjoying as much as you know you should? Do you dread Mondays, spend your free time worrying about your work or feel undervalued by your boss or colleagues? If so, this book is for you.

In this supportive and motivational book Amanda Cullen takes a look at the wide variety of excuses we use which keep us stuck and unhappy in our work. She offers ideas and advice on how to tackle issues so that you can take control, make the necessary changes and transform your working life.

Don't like your colleagues? Spend too long in the office? Not confident in your skills? Or just plain bored? Overcome all of these and many more, and learn how to love your job.

Paperback – ISBN 978-0-9933388-6-1
e-book – ISBN 978-0-9933388-7-8

Also in this series

What's Your Excuse for not Being More Confident?

Charlotta Hughes
Overcome your excuses, increase your confidence, unleash your potential

Do you feel you could achieve much more in life if only you had more confidence? Do you know you'd be happier if you were braver, or had more self-belief? Then this is the book for you.

In this supportive and motivational book former Life Coach of the Year Charlotta Hughes takes a look at all of the ways in which we hold ourselves back and avoid expanding our horizons and she offers advice, ideas and inspiration to help change things.

Scared of failure? Feel unappreciated? Hate change? Worried about what others might think? This book will help you overcome all of your excuses and give you the motivation you need to change the way you feel about yourself.

Paperback – ISBN 978-0-9933388-8-5
e-book – ISBN 978-0-9933388-9-2

Also in this series

What's Your Excuse for not Getting Fit?

Joanne Henson
Overcome your excuses and get active, healthy and happy

Do you want to be fit, lean and healthy, but find that all too often life gets in the way? Do you own a gym membership you don't use, or take up running every January only to give up in February? Then this is the book for you.

This is not yet another get-fit-quick program. It's a look at the things which have prevented you in the past from becoming the fit, active person you've always wanted to be, and a source of advice, inspiration and ideas to help you overcome those things this time around. Change your habits and attitude to exercise for good.

Too tired? Lacking motivation? Bored by exercise? You won't be after reading this book!

Paperback – ISBN 978-0-9933388-0-9
e-book – ISBN 978-0-9933388-1-6